Blues

and

Greens

a produce

worker's

journal

Alan

Chong

Lau

University of

Hawai'i Press

Honolulu

in association with

UCLA Asian American

Studies Center

Los Angeles

D1524508

Printed in the United States of America

05   04   03   02   01   00   5   4   3   2   1

Library of Congress Cataloging-in-Publication Data

Lau, Alan Chong.

   Blues and greens : a produce worker's journal /

   Alan Chong Lau.

      p.   cm. — (Intersections : Asian and Pacific American
      transcultural studies)

ISBN 0 – 8248 – 2210 – 2 (cloth : alk. paper) —

ISBN 0 – 8248 – 2323 – 0 (pbk. : alk. paper)

   1. Produce trade — Poetry.   2. Farm produce — Poetry.

   3. Vegetables — Poetry.   4. Fruit — Poetry.   I. Title.

   II. Intersections (Honolulu, Hawaii)

   PS3562.A7787 B58 2000

811'.54 — dc21   99 – 057298

Front cover photo by John Pai.
Art work courtesy of Francine Seders Gallery, Seattle,
and the artist.

Designed by Bonnie Campbell / Running Feet Books

Printed by the Maple-Vail Manufacturing Group

Contents

iv. hello, little bean sprout!

acknowledgments

MY THANKS TO THE PUBLISHERS of the following works in
which some of these poems first appeared (some in different
versions): *Breaking Silence, An Anthology of Contemporary Asian
American Poets,* edited by Joseph Bruchac (Greenfield Review
Press, 1983); *Image-Prose and Poetry by Northwest Writers* (Seattle
Arts Commission, 1992); "ArtPoetry/Metro, Metro Arts Program
Project," *The Seattle Times,* June 16, 1997; *What Book!? Buddha
Poems from Beat to HipHop,* edited by Gary Gach (Parallax Press,
1998); *Voices of the Community: The West Seattle Cultural Trail,*
edited by Gail Tremblay (Seattle Arts Commission, 1999); *Seattle
Poets and Photographers, A Millennium Reflection* (Seattle Arts
Commission, distributed by University of Washington Press,
1999).

Thanks to everyone who helped me on this project. It's with
great pleasure that I thank the following individuals. Russell
Leong, general editor of University of Hawai'i's Intersections
series, who believed in the book from the beginning and urged
it to completion. Sharon Yamamoto, editor at University of
Hawai'i Press, who supported the project with patience and a
helpful edit. Laureen Mar and Bill Witherup, poet friends who
both took the time to comment and offer suggestions. Thanks
to Aldo Chan for his thoughtful design ideas. Esther Sugai,
Holly Yasui, Elizabeth Aoki, Ferdinand de Leon, Paula Bock,
Bob Shimabukuro, Gary Iwamoto, and Donn Fry, who all took
enough interest in my work to write about it. The dedicated,
sensitive, and talented musicians who played their wonderful

music with my poetry at live readings, Susie Kozawa, Eyvind Kang, and Bob Antolin. Thanks to Masako Ikeda and Elizabeth Hanson for final production help. I also value the support of the late Kay Boyle and of Lawson Inada, Al Corral, Cid Corman, and Gail Tremblay. Thanks to Myong Hee Kim, who gave me the ricepaper I used for the paintings in this book, salvaged from a calligrapher's house after the Kobe earthquake. My best friend, Kazuko Nakane, who has always offered support and criticism when needed. And lastly the customers, co-workers, and supervisors who make up my produce world. We're all in this green boat together.

a blue note

For Wong Fay,
a gentle man,
the produce crew,
and the customers
who made my world.

THE ORIGINS OF THIS BOOK go back over twenty years. It all started when I was laid off from my job as a janitor at a factory that supplied lights for the cockpits of Boeing planes. I fell into a job at an Asian produce market in the International District (Seattle's Asian American neighborhood) quite by chance. In my first few weeks on the job I was in a state of innocent awe at the beautiful colors, textures, and shapes of what I handled. Little images would come to me as I worked and I would jot them down into a notebook I kept in my shirt pocket. Some of the earliest poems in this collection are about the sheer beauty of sliced-open winter melon or stacks of purple-bodied eggplant.

People say that human beings spend most of their waking hours at a job. The work so dominates life that it's hard not to let that become a very real part of your existence. The naive awe I felt over each piece of fruit or vegetable (even in their decomposing states) gradually gave way to a more realistic appraisal of the microcosm I was part of. The interaction between myself with produce, fellow worker, boss, and customer all provided a rich network of experience. Early poems of whimsy were soon joined by moods of disgust, irony, and boredom, giving my world a fuller palette of colors and emotions.

The first draft of this series of poems came about through real urgency. I was asked to give a reading and I only had my notebook of short lines jotted down from work, but these alone were not enough to constitute a full-length poem. My wife helped me arrange these brief snatches of description in a call-and-response dialogue using slogans that had been dutifully posted by each cash register and titled "Ten Commandments of Good Business." I wove these sayings like a frame throughout the poem along with bits of intercom announcements, customer conversations, and produce descriptions. As time went by, more and more images would come to mind to give another dimension to the world of produce.

Although each piece can be read on its own, I feel the poems together create a momentum, a cumulative strength and coherent vision, by being read together side by side. There is an active cross-layering of shapes and sounds and images that work better as they rub off of each other. As the years go by, I find this collection takes on its own identity determined by seasons, hours of the day, days of the week, and people coming and going, never to be seen again.

International District, Seattle, 2000

i.

[blues]

morning blues

Downtown standing on
the manhole cover
this lone figure
a blanket for a cape
enveloped in vapor

Close up
streetlight gleam
off his eyes as bus and man
turn the corner
each going the other way

Sandwiched between
a Vietnamese family
I watch the old woman
peel the skin off an apple
in one motion
her pocketknife tethered to a key chain
as her daughter
wipes the boy's nose
a clean tissue
tugged from a lined pocket

As the trolley lurches
down the hill
to King Street Station
we all jerk forward

Looming ahead
the seagulls scatter
their jumpy squawk
through the fog
it's time to go to work

nappa Harvey Nakaya bean sprouts Eric Kato foo gwa

Jeff Tada takana Terry Nakamura fuki Yamada-san cee gwa

Allan Wong bok choy Ken Louie green onions Kevin Jung

lo bok Andy Shin gai lan Mark Dea sugar peas

Foo Yuen Saechao dong gwa King Man Wong renkon

Steve Goon malungai Hercules Alfredo Durias salayote

Wing Huey Lee jicama Taeyoko Uesugi gobo Todd Hirakawa

udo cilantro lemongrass opo song choy

6 A.M.

From the donut shop
emerges this old-timer
mouth still dusted
with a mustache of powdered sugar

The sweet sweat
of roast pork
from the barbecue shop
collides in an alleyway
of crushed flowers
soaking in yesterday's piss

"All boys up front.

Right away. We need help

at all check stands

immediately."

primping

Before the guy
in the fish department
begins work
he stands in front
of a cracked mirror
adjusting his baseball cap
as steam
rises from a newly tossed
bed of cracked ice
and the eyes of fish
gleam back

going for a dip

In the morning
tails of shrimp
hang limp
around a swimming bowl
of batter

preparing sashimi

From the fish department
the smell
catches us as we clock in
slices the nose
with a blade
of blood soaked in brine

[7]

wintermelon in the shade   LAU

winter melon

Inside each one
hides a snowflake
woven by a spider

nasubi

In the box
sleek purple bodies
washed ashore
gleam and hug each other
to keep from falling

melons

In the bin
the sweet musk
of one sings in the nose

chi goo

The river potatoes
my grandmother once made us
stop the car for
in the California valley heat
dug out of water
fenced in by reeds
now reappear in our produce room
collected in a bamboo basket
somewhere by a river
flowing in the south of China
then flown to L.A.
and tossed in the back of a rig bound for Seattle
it takes longer to recognize
but the taste
the taste is still the same

bitter melon

I like mine overripe
seeds of blood
gleaming under collapsed
yellow

ginger

Ten-year-old Chinese boy
from the shopping cart
borrows this knob of ginger
you make a spacegun

Use the mirror behind
the produce rack
for a screen to hunt down androids
your mother will never see

red delicious

The short white-haired lady
asks me how many apples
make a pound

Weighing them on the scale
I turn around
see fine black hairs
dot her face
scaling a nose
curved in the shell
of an ear
haphazard
where they first fell
from a scissors' clipped dance

It's her
I see on the corner
behind her chair
scissors always aiming up
to where a taller man sits
wrapped in a white cloth

uncovering the evidence

Digging their nails
into the textured cream
that is the flesh
of the taro
They tear open the dry skin
poking the meat
for a firmness

Left behind
dozens of fingerprints
embedded in the tired surface

boys at play

As I enter the back room
there they are
crouched around the desk

Our whole produce crew
staring intently at a strawberry basket
counting down the seconds

How long does it take
a black widow
to wrap threads of gauze
around a wounded wasp's stinger?

They all begin to shout
as the spider twirls
its legs into a dance
"Get him, get him, get him
You bad boy!"

the end of spring

Cherry blossoms
in the gutter
by the beauty shop

this breeze
sends them
underground

Ten Commandments of Good Business

A customer is the most important person in any business.

"Ya see the guy in the jacket? He picked up a box of incense.
I'm still waiting for him to ditch it somewhere.
Then maybe we'll have something."

A customer is not someone to argue or match wits with.

The Vietnamese man has a fondness for a cub scout
cap one size too small.

A customer is a person who brings us his wants. It is our job to
fill these wants.

bean sprouts

Who knows why
the pudgy mama's boy
over by the bean sprouts
wears a half t-shirt
the word "Hunk"
emblazoned across his chest

A customer is not dependent on us, we are dependent on him.

the price

"Why are your sugar peas so cheap?" They all want to know. Well, when they come from Guatemala where peasants pick them for centavos a day — well — we can pass the savings on to you, our shopper.

A customer is not a cold statistic, he is a flesh and blood human being with feelings and emotions like our own.

when it rains

The white man
red bandanna on his head
a wool blanket for a poncho
wears 3D glasses
when it rains

A customer does us a favor when he calls. We are not doing him a favor by serving him.

ii.

[greens]

lotus root & bittermelon touching   LAU

raw peanuts

They come from Beacon Hill or rooms in the District. The callused
feet and cracked heels show a lifetime of walking put to good use.
Knit hats or white kerchiefs pulled over heads shape faces;
lively fingers of each hand toting a bag of special treasure.
They jostle around the bin as the ritual of shopping gives way to
greeting. The produce market is their own private kitchen and we
are the uninvited guests.

"Aieeya, this one is so skinny, the peanut
must be all shriveled up or rotten."

"My, they want 89¢ a pound for this.
Isn't it cheaper on Beacon?"

"Hey, what are you saying?
These peanuts are cheap and they look fresh too."

"Over here where I am. These must be the best peanuts.
He probably just put them out.
The shells aren't so dusty and they're big too."

"Oh really! Then I'll throw these back. I'll be right over."

Some women have been back two or three times
in the course of a day to see if there's been any change.
They encourage us by saying, "Put more out. New one?
Thisee new one?"

Their din permeates the walls, climbs over the Muzak, and
reaches us even in the back room where we trim the
vegetables to the tune from the radio that blares out, "Work
dat sucka to death! I said ah work dat sucka to death, I
said ah work . . . !"

A customer is not an interruption of our work, he is
the purpose of it.

grapes

Grapes are not preferred in bunches. Mothers and grandmothers pluck them off to soothe baby. Young men find them the perfect afternoon snack. Older women distrust anything in groups. Instead make an inspection of each green oval until selection narrows down to a handful of jewels of light trapped inside a plastic bag. Old-timers nimbly finger, mouths suck flesh out. A trail of skins and seeds left anywhere.

A customer is the lifeblood of this and every other business.

stormbringer

Outside
a lone seagull
circles the parking lot
as clouds rob the sky
of any light

"Attention. Will the owner of a white Mazda

in the parking lot please return to your car?

Your lights are on. Thank you!"

the green mustache

He wiggles the bean
under his nose
balanced on his lip
still he can't stop
his son from crying

"Will the customer who wanted dried tamarind

please return to aisle four? Thank you!"

shoplifter

Old woman
caught with a bag of baby shrimp
waits behind the partition

Her husband
finds the only chair available
a bok choy crate
abandoned in front of flats of six-packs
by the loading dock

Stares at the floor
one hand rubbing
a sunken face smooth
the other fingering
the handle of his cane

Waits as the police ask the student cashier
to translate and record
the things that matter

name
address
social security #

When my co-worker
hears the couple's Chinese
he rubs his hand
over a wet apron
clicking his tongue,
"That's bad
That's really bad"

What's left?

Photocopied gray shadows of shrimp
a curved x-ray
the spine of prehistoric vertebrates
and a name
typed neatly on a police report

"Can you call a taxi, please?"
"Yellow cab in five minutes."
"Thank you."
"Thank you."

mustard greens

The long Chinese mustard greens Biceps brings in from
Yotsuya Farms now wave good-bye to me in this shopping cart,
a movable forest driven by this Cambodian family. Their four-
year-old pauses in front of the green onions to imitate tai chi
forms. Outside I see more mustard greens drying up, shriveled
algae on the chain-link fence surrounding a deserted lot.

issei farmer

In winter he comes in, a day-glo orange duck hunter's cap
announcing his arrival. Atop a slight wiry frame in bib
overalls, he's behind the wheel of a green '52 flatbed stacked
high with crates of nashi. Pulling into our loading dock he
says, "This Chevy run good, a real smooth ride." In summer it's
a straw hat and crates of jumbo spinach still dripping from
dawn's harvest. At 75, farming's only a hobby. A younger wife
keeps him alive—that and the Chinese herbs that give him pep
where he needs it.

the gambler's wife

They say she's the gambler's wife. He's dead now but at one time he was a local big shot in pinstripes. He died penniless. Now his widow's careful, always nattily attired in a white wool hat and double-breasted blue coat. It's the cigarette that gives her away. Snug on the corner of her mouth, it hangs by itself protruding from her lip. Her voice churns gravel as she points to a discount piece of bitter melon in a package and says, "Say! Can't you cut this for me? Say! Don't you have anymore, these are all rotten!" When you've brought a box out, she spends an hour picking each one up, turning it around in her hand, holding it up in the light, looking at texture and crispness. After she's jumbled up the whole pile, she'll pick one and only one — usually a small one. Tossing it into her basket, she walks away. The cigarette droops over her lip trailing ribbons of smoke down the aisle.

"Can we have someone from the grocery department
to the loading dock to sign in a delivery? Thank you."

"Hello bok choy bow?"

"Whadda you want, bo lo bow?"

"Gimme one latte, two mocha, and three chicken tail, okay?"

"Okay honey. Five minutes arright."

"Bye bok choy bow!"

"Bye bo lo bow!"

the voice

If you swallowed
a bag of rusty nails
and had an emery board
for a tongue
If your vocal chords
were twisted around bails
of rusty barbed wire
strung across every concentration camp
on the planet
If you had chewed on sand for an eternity
and washed it down with
water from the seven seas
None of these things
would prepare you
for this woman's voice
The way it insinuates itself
under your skin and makes your flesh crawl
batters your eardrum
a garbage can lid
stumbling across a concrete alley
caught on the crumpled lip
of a wheezing dumpster

It's not what she says
it's the sound
of her voice
Rusty razor blades sewn into the rump
of an alley cat doomed to
forage the dumpsites of the world
in search of radioactive mice

this is only a test

Embedded within the spotted
flesh of a papaya
we find a tiny harpoon

The flattened toothpick
of a customer left
in a hurry

the old man remembers asparagus

In the market
spears of asparagus
I once topped by the hundreds
in Toppenish
near the corrugated shed
that led to the valley

My arms
do not carry me far
even stooped over
this walker
that clunks over concrete
I remember another dawn
cooled by ocean waves
a sky of purple
then sunrise

fishing

The small woman's knit cap
barely pokes above our dumpster
a stick she carries
in one hand helps
with a nail on one end
she stabs and pokes
at apples, carrots, and radishes
with a hook on the other end
she pulls in leafy greens of nappa
bok choy and gai choy

Dropping this cornucopia into a gunny sack
she heads down the street
one hand on her stick
the other pulling upward

"Clean up on aisle one,

please. Clean up on aisle one!"

in summer

Fine prickly hair
on the skin
of this winter melon
coated with a chalky dust

In summer
one itches
just to look at it

"50-lb Kokuho on five, please, 50-lb Kokuho on five."

the accident

When the old woman
does a swan dive
between the bean sprouts
and soft bags of poi

We gather around her
on the floor
as she howls in pain

Pointing to a speck
none of us can see
she curses out loud
blames us for her fall

When we hear a week later
that she is suing the store
nobody seems surprised

Omens

1
Lost
chicken foot
pointing to the tree
droops in front
of Anita's Bakery

2
This unwanted yellow hand
a swollen rubber glove
bobs in the sink
circles muddy spinach
picked by Miguel, Manuel or Tomas

3
Found tucked
into the whorled stem
of this crinkly skirt
of gai choy
a customer's car keys

4
Packages of pig's feet
tossed on top of
speckled spheres
of Thai eggplant
point to the gai lan
"Why have you abandoned me?"

5
This nami yam
in the shape of a giant paw
no one wants

as a day goes by
it begins to shrivel
and collapse
into a child's sleepy fist

6
Lean brown legs
doing splits
instant chopsticks
left on the counter

7
The suede jacket
with a ragged collar of fake fur
in fading antelope brown
wraps its torn arms
around a newspaper box
bleeding rust in August
as yellow leaves
stir around it
nervously scratching the pavement

8
Under the tree
stained with cherry blossoms
the teeth of a broken comb

"Attention customers . . . Will the parents of Simon please
come to the front of the store and pick up your son?"

mothra's cousin grazes the produce rack

Am I delirious
or just getting dizzy
off a whiff of the guano
coating these jumbo green beans

Is that an oversized fruit fly
I see with artichoke blade armor?
Pull tab ring dangling from one ear
Feet clad in cherry tomato stem stirrups
His tin pan sombrero
slung casually over one wing
hovering over a forest
of frost white hairs
that sprout off the oblong terrain
of this rotting winter melon
trying to decide
the best entrance to the nectar
of the gods

Either the little guy
overheard Tim telling
one of our more naive customers
that yes, dong gwa
is white watermelon
or this dude's colorblind

Instead I point him
in the direction of an armada
of seedless watermelon
bloody gleaming wedges
of sugar tilted onto
a tundra of chiseled ice
floating on the corner
soliciting thirsty customers
weary of being hot and bothered

"Attention customers, will the person who owns the yellow

Subaru with the license plate 'Fresh Kid Rice' please return

to the parking lot; your motor is running. Thank you."

iii.

[strange root]

strange root

Daikon radish
with six legs of various lengths
that twist & curve up into the clouds,
the peaks of Mt. Huang?

A ginseng root
on steroids?

A curled white pitchfork
turning up soil?

No one wants you
except Mr. Octopus
and even he's too busy
teasing the crabs
in the water tank next door
tentacles curled
around the rubbery tubular necks
of geoducks
shell shackled
by blue rubber bands

"Fives and tens on two please, fives and tens on two!"

paper flowers

No
These aren't crushed carnations
deserted in the gutter
of our produce rack
or paper flowers expanding upward
in a clear glass of water

They are the tension relievers
crumpled wads of white tissue
crushed in the balls
of tiny fists
attached to arms
that poke out of a
white blouse that covers
the curved contours
of an old lady
who tosses a bag full of chicken feet
into the simmering soup pot
as she dusts the photos
of her grandchildren
all smiles in the shadows
of a dresser bureau
against a faded green wall
bathed in a lemony light
filtered through the sagging blades
of the venetian blinds
that tremble in the breeze
of another summer day

"Another cashier up front right away, please!"

the sale on water chestnuts

—— CHINESE NEW YEAR

Not wanting to get hands dirty
the women command me
to dig deeper
into this earth
of muddy curved tubers
miniature tusks that poke out
of a tortoise brown skin
that gleams with
the rub of a thumb

They want the crisp jewel
of sweet meat that crunches juice
hidden in shade
still moist with pond water
at the bottom of this crate
that floated over from China

"Shake shake shake"
they urge with cracked hands
as the embedded dirt rises
to the surface of the International District
and coats us all
in a cloud of dust

matsutake, living treasures under the pine

A musk soaks into your pores. Something that pokes its head from under an icy crust of leaves and pine branches fills the air with a scent that spells autumn. The deer nibble them for snacks.

The Japanese businessman wants to buy them all, squeezing each head, squinting through a magnifying glass the size of a sake cup to check for worms.

The nisei woman says, "Takai takai." Takes an hour to forage through the rack to find the best package while her son looks bored.

The old-timers gather around the specimens, first of the season, and trade stories about their mushroom hunting days before arthritic knees and failed eyesight took their toll. They poke at each one marveling at the size. "Where did they say they got them? Shelton, Cascades, or Port Townsend?" When we tell them they didn't say, they all walk away disappointed.

"Price check on aisle seven, please."

sorting things out

Three grandmas
in baseball caps
with the logos
of moving companies and gas stations
stand in running shoes
crouched over our produce
picking with care
as the overhead scale
trembles to the toss of shoppers

Mouths move
as fingers fly
over this pile of green beans
poured out of a crate
swimming toward open hands

"Will the woman from Asuka Restaurant

please go to the nearest phone. You have a call."

escape from the fish tank

Torso wrapped
in a gauze of dust
This crayfish
from the fish department
crawls out from under
the oranges

With the approach
of my footsteps
he still has the strength
to rear up
pincers spread wide
in defense

garden of eden

This shopping cart
is a stainless steel crib
Nestled on her tummy
on a transparent bag of honey tangerines
this baby lifts her head up
A tiny turtle
that inflates with an intake of breath
to observe the gleam of spotlights
that dance across the color of citrus
and lies down once more
to absorb the color of pictures
that whirl around her head

garden of eden 2

He's not the village idiot
just the herbalist's son
awakened from a night of dreams
sweeter than daylight

Still wrapped in crumpled pajamas
that show Tom chasing Jerry
he shuffles along in slippers
that slap the floor
thinking he's wandered into the garden of eden

Unable to resist any temptation
he takes a bite out of each apple
crushes the juice from a peach
strings garlands of grapes around his neck
and pokes each finger
into the red and orange flesh
of melons exuding the musk
of their valley

Before we can shoo him away
he turns the corner
easing a path through our garden

The percussive crunch of Hi-Ho crackers
turns his head
into a jukebox of slow moans

His ears grin
in scarlet appreciation

Unlike this boy who sleepwalks in bliss
we patrol these fields of merchandise
bored with the process of work
and numb to the textures
of leaf and peel, root and whorl
sinking deep or breaking up
crumbs of earth
rich enough to choke on

"In our fish department today, we have a special on

smoked salmon. Please drop by for a free sample!"

sign language

When our new worker
from Vietnam wants to take a breather
he signals to me

Holding an imaginary stick in mid-air
he snaps it in half
and grins

"Will Yoko Kubinski from Vancouver

please return to the office!"

the king's english

King speaks the king's English
and why not since he's from
the crown colony

When you walk in
off the bus like a zombie
cobwebs of sleep
fogging your head with crumbs of dreams
he's there to wake you up

Brutal but effective
he whispers in your ear
with a grizzled chin
mouthing a coarse whisper
coated with halitosis
as his dentures click like castanets
trying to find their mooring
"You suck, man! Your sook sook all night?"

But when he asks me
if I've seen this new movie
I'm at a loss

Scrunching his face into concentration
he says "How do you say! In Chinese we say,
'teacher again, again, again.'"

It's not until he says
"I likee Marrann Brando"
that I figure it out:
"Godfather III"

the gesture

With an annoyed wave
of her hand
this lady
tells me to get out
of her way without speaking
as she tunnels
through a pile
of blemished bok choy
No single bunch
all good so she finds
individual stalks
still tender
untying each bundle
she scoops up hearts
of green and white
still crisp enough
to come out singing

"Will the customer looking for mochi ice cream

please come up front? Thank you."

"Bharti Kirchner from Speedee Travel, please go to the

nearest phone and pick up line six. You have a phone call."

the meat of a mango

He doesn't eat this overripe mango
as much as devour it
slitting the discolored sagging wrinkles
of skin he turns the peel
inside out as his mouth
latches onto it
in sucking surge of power
a vacuum cleaner in steady motion
The sweet succulence
of flesh
is drained in seconds
The orange gush
of pulp in a wet gleam
spread over the salt & pepper
stubble of his chin
drips juice
staining his apron
with dark tears of sugar
and a profusion of the tropics
he'll never see

All that remains
is a flat football
of a pit
sporting a strained coat
of troll wet hair
that once grew
through the meat
of a mango

iv.

[hello, little bean sprout!]

sprout woman

The woman who delivers bean sprouts works hard. Plastic bags of fragile water trapped in all these crunchy seeds of mung and soy.

The Koreans take the soy sprouts and add red pepper to fleck it with heat. The Japanese blanch the bean sprouts quickly and toss in a suribachi of toasted sesame seeds that always get caught between the teeth. And they never forget the shoyu. The Vietnamese sprinkle them raw over steaming bowls of pho tinged with the breath of red basil. The Chinese use them both in stir-fry and soup.

Every day this woman is on the phone to take your order. Brushes back the hair that mats on her forehead in a steam-filled warehouse out in the Rainier Valley.

When I pick up the phone, I can hear her shout out instructions in Chinese to her crew as the roar of traffic and the splash of water crackles in the background, "Oh Alan, this is bean sprout!" As she delivers her tender cargo in a beat-up tan van scraped with rusty scars, you'll see mounds of sprouts in bags stacked neatly in banana boxes that crisscross on top of one another.

Sometimes she's frustrated: "I work to pay for their education but now the big one says she don't want to go to school any-more. What can I do?"

The smallest one with a mop of black hair cropped in bangs yells out "Hello watermelon!" as her sturdy brown hand holds out an invoice pad specked with water. As she leaves, I reply, "Bye little bean sprout!" Someday she will wear red lipstick, march in the Chinese Girls Drill Team, and I won't recognize her.

Other times the bean sprout woman will notice the crisp dark green stalks of gai lan as she goes out the door wheeling a hand truck. Comes back to pick out a bunch with chubby fingers for her family's supper.

One morning, I ask her how she got married. She tells me with a smile, "I waited a few years after his proposal thinking it over. One night at Tai Tung's I just decided to go with fortune. 'The person sitting across from you will be your future partner.'"

"100-lb Elephant on two please, 100-lb Elephant."

plumbing the depths

It is the plump notes these women hope
will answer back

Their fingers
a quick snap
against fat legs
of white daikon

late summer

When it's been in the sun
long enough
who's to tell the difference
between a half-eaten pineapple
and the head of a sunflower
bending down to drink shadow

the footprint

The pattern
of a man's sole
crushed into
a daikon leaf
dropped in the parking lot

old daikon   tops & stems—

green onions

Sitting down to supper
the smell of a day's work
still rises from
my stained hands
to fill our soup bowl

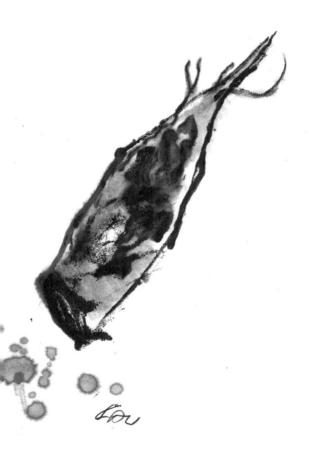

black iris

This banana peel
on blacktop
torched by the heat
curls upward

"Fives and tens on check

stand two, please—

I need some fives and tens

right away, please."

Scavengers

These thin dark men
eyes with the warmth of coals
that glow under the brim
of their grease-stained baseball caps
ricochet directions in Spanish

To them deep sea diving into a pile
of refuse
is no mere hobby

They search for buried treasure
we toss without looking
bruised cheeks of tomatoes
clusters of green that
can be re-bunched into respectability
even the withered face
of old man pepper
is restored again

What we know
means nothing to them
Airline bags stitched with safety pins
bulge under the weight

Running down the street
to the tavern
they're off to set up
their own market
for the poor and hungry

"Will the kids from Renton please line up

in the parking lot. Your bus is waiting to go."

the sore loser

On a lunch break
I hear the repeated howl
of a drinker 86ed
from the corner tavern
As the wind blows debris
that turn circles in the middle of the street
he begins to cry
"The guy behind the counter is a bastard!
The guy behind the counter is a bastard!
The guy behind the counter is a bastard!"
all the time shuffling his feet
and throwing jabs
with small fists
raised toward the sky
as clouds slowly shift toward the water
in scuds of gray

"Please stop by our produce department
and see our new assortment of plants
including wisteria, bamboo, and orange."

the gate

Entering Chinatown
it's not stone lions
on either side that greet me
but two guys
in baseball caps
caught in a simultaneous yawn
by the bus stop
across from Union Station

this sky

This sky
the ribs of
a blue clam shell
stretches over Elliott Bay

starting work

The charcoal squawk of crows
from their perch
on the Publix Hotel
sprays a gray sky
with greetings
off this roof of morning

While seagulls
practice flight patterns
down the street
across from an empty lot
drop their drippy frosting
on "Piece of Cake" below

the apology

Bumping into a customer
I turn around to apologize
find only the leafy grin
of Mr. Nappa snug
in his wooden crib

tools of his trade

My friend Vinh
stops by the produce rack
with a square briefcase
covered in Naugahyde skin

Coordinator of a safe sex workshop
he places the container
on top of tubers of lotus root
to show me the tools of his trade

Opening the lid
he reveals an assortment
of flesh-toned rubber penises
A swarm of eels
trapped inside a tank
with no place to run

baby ruth

He pulls the change
for his purchase
out of the murky folds
of a creased plastic bag

It's not that he can't speak
This old-timer
the curve of his back
defines the yellow windbreaker
that drapes his torso

He sits at the table
in our deli and chews
intent on his candy bar
oblivious to the crusted petal
of blood that starts from the lip
and veers off his chin

The smooth sculpted sheen
of cheekbone and drowsy eye
partially hidden under a fedora
with a flake of red feather
for a stop sign

finding the hair of a mexican woman in this box of sugar peas

I put the lemongrass out
stripping the dried stems
off each stalk

With each tear
a lemony mist
scents the air around us

As we work Ahn tells me
in his country
lemongrass grows in the backyard
a natural fence to
keep snakes away

I find your long hair
curled around the stem
of a sugar pea
as I pour out
their flat green bodies
in a pile

I wish I could
twist these stems
of lemongrass
into a fragrant skirt
for you to wear
and keep the slither
of snakes from rustling
around your sturdy ankles
as you pluck each pod
off vine after vine after vine

the raft

Earwig
you cling to
this raft of baby bok choy
in the froth
of a brown churning sea
fed by the chatter
of a faucet

Tell me
where this journey
takes us?

a view from the stairs

Piles of bird poop
on the blue tiles
This lone weed begins to blossom

boredom

With nothing to do
Kiyoshi carves a dick
out of the snow white flesh
of a daikon

Tops it off
with veins any junkie would envy
They skirt the vertical circumference
swimming toward the glans

As he sculpts, he laughs
tells me of the time
he took a job
guiding a busload of Japanese farmers
enthusiastic to tour
the day-to-day operations
of a Mexican asparagus farm

In the evening
he discovers the real purpose
behind this south-of-the-border excursion

Reduced to translator
he's the farmers' go-between
while they haggle over rates
at a whorehouse

As the story ends
he returns to his sculpture
undermining it all
with a garnish
of tiny red radish
he chooses for the balls

the river, the potatoes

The women who come in the afternoon
are younger than the grandmothers
who wait for the doors to open
in the morning
when the only thing
that stirs around our parking lot
are crows hopping
and the clean-up guy
that ushers debris into
a sliced up oil can
with a worn broom handle

Heads bowed over
the cold contours of a sewing machine
at the factory all day
they are here now
ready to shop for dinner

Their laughter recalls earlier days
as girlfriends on a picnic
by the lake with the pavilion

One by one what's on display
is dismantled, plastic cartons
are tossed aside
useless as the stumps
of fallen trees

They pour the river potatoes
out into our container
so that their hands
may travel freely over each nub,

horn and speckled fat body
Their fingers are water
that wash over every pebble
in the muddy stream

As a friend
cuts in front
obscuring her point of focus
one woman doesn't hesitate
to let her know

In her saltiest dialect
she shrieks for all to hear
"You stinky old cunt,
out of my way!"

after the rain

After the rain
this jewel of fire
the sun shimmers through

a water drop
that trembles off the lip
of this trash can
on the corner

V.

[long beans and
the maori warrior]

long beans and the maori warrior

As I exit the bus
I look up to see that
with a few deft touches of the pen
someone has transformed
the face of TR the millwright
"Metro Maintenance Worker of the Year"
into a Maori warrior

At my stop
Poy the bus driver
wants to know why
he can't find long beans

Feet on the sidewalk
I yell back that it's winter
and they have to come
all the way from Mexico

"Will customer Yong Soon Min

please come to the Shiseido cosmetics counter?"

the squeak of sugar peas

The squeak
of sugar peas
rubbing pod against pod
stirred through
by the hands of a person
who knows

every day
when the doors open
our vegetables
stand for inspection
dripping water

the return of the gambler's wife

The first thing I see
next to my shoes
is the hem of a tattered blue coat
covering pajamaed feet
stuffed into bedroom slippers
at rest on the metal pads
of a rented wheelchair
that squeaks as it moves

The voice
that once growled
now comes out of a shrunken face
that swallows back
a feeble moan
as she points
a limp finger
at each item
her hand can't reach

as a friend pushes her away
I already know

frost warning

1
Plastic bread clips
clicking notes in the wind
dance colors of red yellow and blue
on the chain-link fence

winter washes my face again
with cold cracked hands

2
The way
wind arranges these leaves
over a storm grate
for a moment

3
the leaf
dressed in frost
pinned down by a fence
still vibrates

4
Wings shiver
legs circle
in a twitch of reflex
This young moth lost
in the coiled heart
of a leafy green
from Oxnard
too weak to fly

5
Around the corner
coming out of the brick
in a spider web of dust
studded with cigarette butts

three purple flowers

"The owner of Shiro's Restaurant,

please go to the nearest phone and pick up line five?

Thank you."

the argument

A brush of shopping carts
and words are exchanged

The immigrant from Japan says,
"Why don't you go back where you came from?"
The immigrant from China replies,
"Why don't you go back where *you* came from?"

Shopping for vegetables
I wonder why
we are always searching
for a place called home

"50-lb Niko Niko on five please."

three lumpy oranges

At dumpster's bottom
three lumpy oranges
cool off
in a pool of fish blood

three lumpy oranges   lew

bunching gai lan

Cutting across
dark green leaves
in a zigzag of hunger
I see the worm
has left his signature

the spill

Upset at the spill
yet the mosaic
on the floor
leaves of purple cabbage
scattered through match sticks
of green onion tops
blink colors
off a white floor

perfection in design

I could be in an airplane
stunned by earth's natural formations
in some sun-baked desert

Instead in this shopping cart
it's the swirl
of a baby's newly shaven head

the kids from tokyo

The boy
with hair
streaked the tint
of lime green Jell-O
caresses his skateboard
with one hand
and grabs an azuki bean Popsicle
with the other
as his girlfriend
waits by his side
worrying her nose rings
with the tip of her finger
painted frost pink

the interrogation

The man with a back
bent in the shape of a
curved coat hanger
is better today

Not needing a walker
he turns his shopping cart around
barricades himself
in our discount corner

With the patience of an attorney
he questions
the motive of every bruised banana
speckled with birthmarks

examines the evidence
of every yellow finger
curved to withered black
torn from the comfort of bunched company

ID at dusk

Firecrackers crackle
snaps of sound
off the chain-link fence
by the Chong Wa Playground

The Chinese Girls Drill Team
strut their strident walk
cutting turns off
in unison razor precision
and boys shoot hoop
waiting for that whoosh
of perfection
to echo off the blacktop

Down the alley
Donnie Chin in IDEC khakis
flashlight staring down an alleyway
checks on a stalled car
as the sun brushes
colors across the pavement
before fleeing the scene

the fight

Two overweight men
sway against the pavement
by the Red Front Tavern
t-shirts torn
and blood wearing their heads
for crowns

Two cops apply handcuffs
One looks bored
the other
can't stop giggling
as the crowd begins to
file back into the comfort
of the dark
and the glow of a TV set
looming over a counter
that sags under the weight
of fifteen bottles of tired beer

in front of the bank

This woman stands in front
of the bank crying

On the corner
a man draws wings
for an angel
on a cardboard box

The broken thumb
of spring
does a clumsy skip
around the block

"Please drop by our grocery department

for a free sample of a new product,

mochi ice cream in five delicious flavors.

On sale now for a limited time."

orphan

At this bus stop
a single blade of green onion
broken off a bunch
that belongs
to the bag
cradled by the puffy hands
of an old woman
somewhere on a bus
rattling toward Genesee

"Attention! Loomis is here. Loomis is here."

her brown face

Eyebrows knit
she trims the swamp cabbage
with one foot balanced on a bok choy crate
by the Bush Hotel

I would take
the delicate green leaves
shaped like the tips of spears
snap them off their hollow stems
one by one

and make a wreath
to wrap around her hands
that have forgotten how to bend

Her brown face
takes this sword of the sun
to dance light
around the whole block

day of the parade

Sunday, February 27, 1983, after the
death of 13 people at Wah Mee in Seattle's
Chinatown / International District

1
The first truckload
jars sleep loose
Nappa from California
insists its importance
with this crate splattered with mud
and stamped with a single boot print

The light in the fields
forces worms to hide
in this boxed forest
of leafy shade

Trimming leaves
overgrown stalks
come out of hearts
layers of green veins
converge into a mush of pus
that smears my apron

Today's shoppers lack excitement
Circle past oranges
gleaming six pounds for a dollar
Ignore the presence of
a tangled chorus of bean sprouts
that sing water
Resist the temptation to stroke
long white legs of daikon or dig their nails
into the firm flesh of winter melon

instead repeat a refrain
underscored by supermarket Muzak
"When's the Chinatown parade,
do you know?
Do you speak English?"

2
An empty tour bus
runs over the offering
of vegetables arranged on a sidewalk
to appease the lion

Already people
anticipating the parade
maneuver the bricks of Hing Hay Park
strewn with tossed leftovers
for pigeons and seagulls

It doesn't matter whether it's good cheap food
or dots of blood
that blemish a doorway

Some peer down the alley
where police stumbled
"into a sea of blood"

3
The next morning
nobody I talked to
knew there was a parade
Some only saw it as a bad dream
coming into their living rooms
on the evening news
to rob their sleep

All over this city
other people fill space
empty of curiosity
Mourn a loss
that silences the ground
where no offerings can ever penetrate
no birds can ever settle

What is real
repeats itself 13 times
Reverberates through families
an unwanted history
burning in an unlit closet
for generations to choke on

"Good evening, shoppers. The store will be closing

in fifteen minutes.

Please bring all items up to the front.

Thank you and have a nice evening."

green tamarind John Richard Keoni Gaudiz Corpusz mizuna

Alan Kimura opo Randy Rolando Beza kumquat

Alesander Andrews moqua Ken Huei lobok Carey Law

takenoko Tim Burris asparagus Marc Yamada kyuri

Dave Nakamura salayote Emmanuel Juta hon shimeji Rey Lobo

shishito yucca Nhon Lam chayote Michael Williams taro

Erik Sommers satsuma imo yam David Lynam shiitake

Brian Baba saba banana Phoun Nguyen enoki green papaya

swamp cabbage kang kong horseradish

"WORK THAT SUCKA TO DEATH, I SAID WORK THAT
SUCKA TO DEATH . . . "

a funny word

He knows
it must be funny
when this boy
compares the size
of a baby taro
to the dimensions of his own

"Chin chin" he says
This shiny toy of a word
he puts on display
Glad for his parents attention
when they laugh

Words he can't stop saying
the sound
a wish for simple pleasure

two women talking

This waitress coming home from work still wears her black
vest over a white blouse. The sheen of cooking grease coats her
front pockets, once swollen with the weight of an order pad.
Chubby fingers dart through the air as she translates for a
friend who beams at every word.

In accordion folds, the first panel has two tulips that cover
the space like wild flowering trees. Below this is a woman in a
pink dress between a plane too low to the ground and a sinking
bus. The words read "If I could give you something special, it
would be a vacation." The next panel has a huge orange couch
that threatens to swallow up two female figures, one small
and one large. Above this is scrawled, "My favorite time is
when we read together."

Getting off at Third and Union, I barely make out the last panel
divided by two curved lines that meet at a V in the middle of
the page. That must be a giant bird flying off to a new land as
yet undiscovered.

the boy and the jackfruit

Gigantic larvae
the skin
a lumpy landscape
studded with dull thorns

Inside yellow petals of chewy flesh
that pull apart
around brown nutty seeds

The guy from
our travel bureau
stares at this cross section
of sticky fruit
lost in memory

"When I see this
I remember my mother
in the market
as she scoured stalls
for the round pregnant shape
that guaranteed sugar

I would sell it for her
around the neighborhood
each piece on a tray
Chunks of sweet sunlight
to chew away heat
This was my job
When I was a boy"

Years later
they ran across fields
He still can't forget
how he bent down to the muddy water

As he turned around
so many bodies
bobbing in unison
tangled in weeds
by a crumbling shore

when work lets out

In the shadow
of the International Realty sign
the little boy
is taller than his dad now

Squatting
on the slope
a man feeds his only son
red grapes
that are seedless
one by one
waits for him
to chew, then swallow
this throat of a baby bird
trembles in the wind

All around town
cars drive by
never stopping
as a dark envelope of sky
smears streaks of reds and blues
over the cherry trees
on the hill
overlooking the bay
where hazy crumbs of light
will soon become stars
to guide the trawlers home

coming home

The sun shines
on the other side
of the street today

I've got
the dirt of China
underneath my nails

Tonight the musk
of water chestnuts
buried in water
sinks deep
into my dreams

Slivers of light
skimming off this bowl of morning
discarded moans of ancestors
and torn cries of antelope
fade off into the distance

Footprints that earth cannot hold
sounds the wind will not carry

self-portrait   LAU

about the author

ALAN CHONG LAU WAS BORN July 11, 1948, and grew up in Paradise, California. He received a B.A. in art from the University of California at Santa Cruz. He is the author of *The Buddha Bandits Down Highway 99* (with Garrett Hongo and Lawson Inada, 1976), and he published a book of poetry, *Songs for Jadina*, in 1980. His work has appeared in many publications.

Lau has taught in the University of Washington's Asian American Studies Department, the Poet-in-the-Schools program at Rainier Beach, and at the Nathan Hale School in Seattle.

He is the recipient of a special projects grant from the California Arts Council (1978); a Creative Artist Fellowship for Japan administered by the Ministry of Culture in Japan, the Japan/U.S. Friendship Commission, and the National Endowment for the Arts (1993); and a Seattle Art Commission Grant (1994). In 1981 he won the American Book Award. He has served on the board of the Wing Luke Asian Museum and as arts editor for the *International Examiner*, an Asian American community newspaper in Seattle. Lau is also a visual artist and has been represented by the Francine Seders Gallery of Seattle since 1980. His work has been exhibited in the U.S., Japan, and England.

Alan Chong Lau continues to work daily in an Asian produce department in Seattle's International District.